Put 'em up!
Put 'em up!
Bert

TERRY:
I MISS you
already!
SHIRLEY

I'll get you,
my pretty,
And give you a
good petting
Maggie

You warm this
Tin Man's
heart!
Jack

Kid, you're
a trouper!
Ray

I, TOTO

ACKNOWLEDGMENTS

*A very special thanks to Toto's
honorary guardians:*

Tod Robert Machin, Woolsey Ackerman,
Elaine Willingham, Tina Cassimatis,
Steve Cox, Ned Comstock, Tom Wilhite

*And, an extra special thanks
from me and Toto to:*

Alice Spitz

Background illustrations: Page 1: Detail from original art by W. W. Denslow for The
Songs of Father Goose, *sheet music, 1900. Page 2: Illustration by John R. Neill (with a
nod to original Oz illustrator W. W. Denslow) from* The Road to Oz, *1909. Pages 3-4:
Illustration by John R. Neill from* The Road to Oz, *1909.*

Published in 2001 by
Stewart, Tabori & Chang, a Company of La Martinière Groupe
115 West 18th Street, New York, NY 10011

Library of Congress Cataloging-in-Publication Data.
Carroll, Willard.
    I, Toto: the autobiography of Terry, the dog who was Toto/by Willard Carroll;
designed by Timothy Shaner.
    p. cm.
    "A Linda Sunshine book."
    ISBN 1-58479-111-X
    1. Terry (Dog) 2. Dogs—United States—Biography. 3. Toto (Fictitious character) I.
Title.

PN1995.9.A5 C37 2001
791.8'092'9—dc21
    [B]   2001034189

PHOTO CREDITS: Photographs from the Willard Carroll collection by Richard Glenn.
Selected photographs of Carl Spitz, his family and kennels, originally owned by
Hango Dennison. Reprinted courtesy of the family. Other photographs courtesy
of the Academy of Motion Picture Arts and Sciences, the Academy Foundation,
Margaret Herrick Library, Photobition Burbank and the Willard Carroll collection.

Printed in Hong Kong
10 9 8 7 6 5 4 3 2 1
First Printing

I, TOTO

The Autobiography of Terry,
the Dog who was Toto

by Willard Carroll

*Designed by
Timothy Shaner*

A Linda Sunshine Book

Stewart, Tabori & Chang
New York

Haaken

Claire

This book is dedicated
to my faithful companions
— past and present —
along the yellow brick road:

*Star, Toto, Solitaire, Haaken, Claire,
Molly, Barty, Hatty, Romy*
and *Tom*
(who, by the way, is not a dog
but who knows a thing-or-two
about unconditional love)

Toto

Solitaire

Barty & Hatty

Romy

Molly

"It was Toto that made Dorothy laugh
and saved her from growing as gray
as her other surroundings."
—L. FRANK BAUM

"Any dog, trained as Carl Spitz trains them,
cannot fail to become man's best friend."
—CLARK GABLE

"I firmly believe that humans could well
afford to stop a minute now and then and
think just how fine it is to have companions
and friends as loyal, trusting, courageous
and, above all, as intelligent as dogs."
—CARL SPITZ

"Without the help of the dog—no world!"
—ZENDAVESTA

INTRODUCTION

July 27, 1993. The San Fernando Valley in Southern California. The stretch of Ventura Freeway, which passes through North Hollywood, was undergoing a much-needed lane expansion.

Late morning. I parked my car behind the Riverside Drive address I had been given and walked on newly overturned earth. In the early stages of making a four-lane freeway into six, construction vehicles and workers toiled. The hard hats didn't notice me, and I didn't pay much attention to them.

A bulldozer moved a small pile of dirt and rock from one area of the site to a larger pile. I walked to the mound, kicked at the rubble, and thought, "This is where the dog learned her routines. This is where 'Terry' set off to work one day and returned as 'Toto.' This is where Toto lived a happy life. And somewhere around here is where Toto died and was buried."

At just that moment—and feeling a bit sad about the death some fifty years before of one of the most famous canines of all time—the rubble shifted a bit, covering one of my shoes with pebbles and dust.

I pulled the shoe out from under the stones and gave the mound a little nudge. My foot struck something solid. Not dirt, not rock, not bones, but tin—something made of tin. And no, not a rusty tin man!

It was a nine-inch square metal box that protruded out from the mound. I picked it up, dusted it off, and tried to pry open the top. But it wouldn't budge. I took the box back to my car and, using my car key, pried open the tin lid. I looked inside. . . .

But I'm getting ahead of myself.

December 13, 1959. 6:00 PM The second TV airing of THE WIZARD OF OZ *on CBS.*

That evening, I watched the movie for the first time in the living room of my family's house in Easton, Maryland. I was four. We had a 21-inch state-of-the-art, black-and-white console television. No one we knew had color; everybody was waiting for it to be 'perfected.'

I watched the movie not from a chair, or a sofa, or the floor, but riding atop a spring-action rocking horse, keeping pace on the plastic steed for the entire two hours—faster and faster during the action and musical moments, appropriately measured for the more somber ones. (To this day, I can only watch TV in perpetual motion, although I long ago traded in my rocking horse for a series of rocking chairs.)

It would be seven more years and as many annual viewings before I would see OZ in color (either it had at last been perfected or we could finally afford it.) Two major memories of that first childhood viewing of the MGM film stay with me: that the Wicked Witch of the West was

OPPOSITE: *Rules booklet from* The Wonderful Game of Oz, *Parker Brothers, 1921.* ABOVE RIGHT: TV Guide, *December 13, 1959.* RIGHT: *Myself at age four, in TV-watching mode.*

extraordinarily terrifying (it's been reported that I would dismount the plastic pony and flee the room at her every appearance) and that Toto was the real star of the movie.

Toto, Dorothy's faithful, somewhat scruffy-looking dog is in virtually every scene of the film. (Toto is actually in more scenes than Judy Garland, though the dog doesn't have as many close-ups. There are only nine shots in which Terry has the screen completely to herself.) And she's the catalyst for the incredible adventure the film delivers. Dorothy wants to get back to Kansas, of course, but it was her profound love and devotion to her dog that carried the greatest emotional weight for me. And, of course, Toto's feelings for Dorothy were mutual. I was convinced.

Later, when I read the L. Frank Baum book, I would see that—opposite of what normally occurs in a book-to-screen adaptation—Toto was actually a more fully developed character in the movie. Instead of the somewhat passive, along-for-the-ride companion in the book, the MGM Toto is an integral, active participant in moving the plot along. (I always bristle when people refer to the main characters in *The Wizard of Oz* as the "famous four." In my mind, they number FIVE).

I would later learn that the name of the cairn terrier who played Toto was Terry. And what a performer! Everything you could ask for in an actor. The fact that this particular actor was a dog struck me, even as a four-year-old, as irrelevant.

Try to think of *The Wizard of Oz* without that pooch's expression of fear when Miss Gulch forces her into the basket or that look of joy when she is reunited—a couple of times—with Dorothy. And that voice! Truly Terry/Toto had a bark like no other. *(Note for those triviaholics: Toto barks 44 times in the movie.)*

As I grew older and learned more about how movies were made, I found tons of information about the biped stars of *The Wizard of Oz*. But very little was available about Toto. So, in between my professional life—writing and directing movies—I decided to find out as much as I could about Toto.

And this is what I found. . . .

In reference books, disappointingly little attention is paid to canine performers other than Lassie or Rin Tin Tin. Toto is nowhere to be found on the Internet Movie Database—the indispensable web tool. Search for 'Toto' and up pops a cross-reference for an Italian actor by that name. But a dog? Not even a footnote.

I knew that Terry/Toto had been trained by Carl Spitz, who died in 1976. There was a paragraph or two about Spitz in the numerous making-of volumes devoted to *The Wizard of Oz*. With the help of several archivists and fellow travelers in the Oz world, I amassed a considerable collection of photographs, clippings and information. But where was the personal story? I knew scattered details of Toto's career but not what kind of life the dog led away from the movie business. What was it like for a canine star of the 1930s? And where was she buried?

I discovered that several of Carl Spitz's animals had been interred at the Camarillo Pet Cemetery in Ventura, California. A visit there and a perusal of their records, however, showed no Terry or Toto among the permanent residents.

Where to look next? Of course, the obvious often eludes us and, as I was driving home from the pet cemetery I thought, "Why not try the phone book?"

In the local North Hollywood directory I found a listing for Alice Spitz, Carl Spitz's

ABOVE: Carl Spitz's dog training instruction record from the 1950s.
OPPOSITE: Dorothy and Toto in Oz.

widow. I made a call, introduced myself, and asked if she cared to talk about her husband's work and a certain canine.

"How about now?" she asked.

I was at her home in twenty minutes.

Alice Spitz was in her eighties, but the memories of her husband's dog-training days were fresh and vivid.

In the early 1930s, Southern California's San Fernando Valley was a wide-open basin with orange groves that stretched for miles. Ranches sprawled from North Hollywood to the San Gabriel Mountains. Over the next two decades, the orange groves were pushed farther and farther towards the distant mountains while the scent of citrus was replaced by automobile exhaust. Valley homes in the path of concrete progress were sacrificed; one of those was the home and kennel of animal trainer Carl Spitz.

A German-born immigrant, and one-time fireman, Spitz possessed a profound love of animals and an innate understanding of them. Since 1919, he had occupied himself with training dogs. His primary achievement, up to that time, had been perfecting a style of silent dog commands to be used by the deaf. Departing a Depression-scarred homeland, Spitz arrived in New York in 1926, moved almost immediately to Chicago, and then, just as quickly, headed for Los Angeles.

In late 1927, Spitz's Hollywood Dog Training School, located on Riverside Drive in North Hollywood, opened to the public. "At this time," according to Carl Spitz, "the training of dogs for the public was, in general, considered nonsense."

Spitz was decidedly a pioneer in the training of dogs, and his methods were anything but nonsense. Much of his common-sense emphasis on

ABOVE: Carl Spitz with Buck at the intercom and (below) the tub at the kennel. RIGHT: A page from Carl Spitz's dog training manual.

HOLLYWOOD DOG TRAINING SCHOOL

CARL SPITZ, Owner and Trainer

WE ALL KNOW THAT ANY HUMAN BEING, WHETHER HE WANTS TO BECOME A MECHANIC, SALESMAN OR SCIENTIST, MUST FIRST ATTEND GRAMMAR SCHOOL. IN GRAMMAR SCHOOL HE LEARNS HOW TO READ AND WRITE - HOW TO THINK AND STUDY. HE LEARNS THE RELATIONSHIP BETWEEN CAUSE AND EFFECT AND THE MEANING OF DISCIPLINE. ONLY AFTER A PERSON HAS MASTERED THE FUNDAMENTALS HE LEARNS IN ELEMENTARY SCHOOL CAN HE ADVANCE TO MORE SPECIALIZED STUDIES.

OUR FOUR-LEGGED PAL, THE DOG, MUST ALSO UNDERGO ELEMENTARY SCHOOLING. HE MUST BE WELL-TRAINED IN THE FUNDAMENTAL OBEDIENCE COURSE BEFORE HE CAN BE TRAINED TO BE A HUNTER, COMPANION TO THE BLIND, ASSISTANT TO THE POLICE OR A MOTION PICTURE STAR.

THE FUNDAMENTAL OBEDIENCE COURSE TEACHES OUR DOG A GROUP OF COMMANDS WHICH HE SHOULD KNOW AND EXECUTE REASONABLY WELL ON DEMAND. MOST IMPORTANT, THE FUNDAMENTAL OBEDIENCE COURSE INSTILS A SENSE OF DISCIPLINE IN OUR DOG.

IN THE HIGHER CLASSES OF TRAINING WE APPEAL INCREASINGLY TO OUR DOG'S INHERITED ABILITIES AND INSTINCTS, HIS SENSE OF SMELL, COURAGE, TEMPERMENTAL SOUNDNESS, INTELLIGENCE AND ALERTNESS. LET US BE PARTICULARLY AWARE OF THIS FACT - IF THE DOG'S FUNDAMENTAL OBEDIENCE TRAINING IS DEPENDABLE AND GOOD, ANY ADVANCED TRAINING WILL BE EQUALLY GOOD.

THE SPIRIT OF A DOG...HIS DESIRE TO WORK AND TO OBEY COMMANDS...IS IMPORTANT. NEVER TRY TO MAKE EITHER A MECHANICAL PUPPET OR AN ANGEL OF HIM. ALWAYS KEEP HIM ENJOYING HIS WORK, EVEN IF HE IS A LITTLE BIT DEVILISH, BUT REQUIRE HIM TO WORK ACCURATELY.

. . . .

discipline tempered with kindness—detailed in his 1938 book, *The Training of Dogs,* and today accepted as manifest—was new at the time. His valley kennel was state-of-the-art when there were hardly any other practitioners of the art.

Borderline luxurious, Spitz's kennels boasted spacious quarters for the animals, with a large porcelain dog tub for washing. There was a specially-constructed area for training police dogs, and a small pool was added later to prepare his future movie dogs for water work. Spitz even had a cumbersome intercom system connecting the house and kennel so that at night, if the dogs barked, he could whistle through the system to quiet them.

Almost immediately upon his arrival in Los Angeles, the trainer's talents were put to use in the movies. The handful of silent films on which Spitz cut his teeth gave way to "talkies" and, with that transition, Spitz's verbal commands to the animals had to be silenced. Adjusting swiftly, Spitz called upon his experience in Germany—training dogs for the deaf—to work out a series of soundless but effective visual cues.

Spitz's first sound film assignment was the Al Jolson movie *Big Boy* in which the trainer directed two Great Danes. He followed this up with the 1930 John Barrymore *Moby Dick* (and, no, he didn't train the whale). Carl Spitz suddenly found himself in significant demand as the virtuoso handler of film dogs.

Many more high-profile assignments followed: Prince Carl was the Great Dane in *The Most Dangerous Game* (a movie shot simultaneously with and on many of the same sets as *King Kong*). Buck was Clark Gable's Saint Bernard in *Call of the Wild* and the first "star" to emerge from Spitz's group of canines. After *Call of the Wild,* Buck appeared in several more films and made many stage appearances at film feature presentations, dog shows, and other exhibitions.

Later notables would be Prince in *Wuthering Heights,* Musty in *Swiss Family Robinson,* and Mr. Binkie in *The Light that Failed.* Fluff, Lucky Dog, and Firefly were among the other dogs in the Spitz kennel who worked frequently at the

LEFT: Detail from the original brochure for the Swedish release of the MGM film, 1940.

major and minor studios. But it would be a tiny, at-first painfully shy, female cairn terrier who would eclipse all the other dogs in his stable. Ultimately, even the world-famous Buck would be displaced as the reigning canine star of the Hollywood Dog Training School.

The little cairn was named Terry, and she came to Carl Spitz in 1933 in desperate need of training. Exasperated with their own failed attempts, her Pasadena owners deposited the timid cairn terrier at the school. Spitz put Terry through his standard regimen of absolute—though not harsh—training and, in a few weeks, she was no longer a threat to the carpeting. In another year, she would be starring opposite Shirley Temple. Ultimately, Terry would appear in a dozen or so films and achieve immortality as a cultural icon in *The Wizard of Oz*.

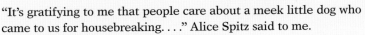

"It's gratifying to me that people care about a meek little dog who came to us for housebreaking. . . ." Alice Spitz said to me.

"And ended up a legend," I added.

Alice Spitz nodded. "Carl would be so very happy. He once said that one of the saddest experiences of life is outliving our dogs. It's good to remember them. To honor them."

I nodded in agreement.

Mrs. Spitz provided me with the exact address of the original kennel—12350 Riverside Drive. She explained that in 1958, when the Ventura Freeway was first being built, Carl Spitz had been forced to relocate, vacating the original kennel property, which was quickly plowed under and built over.

And, most significantly, she revealed to me that somewhere on that plot of ground Toto had been laid to rest some fifty years earlier.

After leaving this gentle woman—who visibly enjoyed the pleasing reminiscences of her and her husband's dog-filled past— I drove to the original location of Carl Spitz's Hollywood Dog Training School, thinking about the legacy of the MGM movie.

The Wizard of Oz is one of those rare movies that occupies space in both our conscious and unconscious. In many ways, the movie visualization of *Oz*, a dream, has become a sort of collective vision, an exciting, oddly soothing "movie dream" tucked away securely in our own dreams.

We respond to the brilliant surface fantasy, of course, but it's the relationships between Dorothy and "the best friends anybody ever had" that propel us to return.

And then, of course, there's Toto. And that special, unconditional love of a lonely child for her little dog. And vice-versa. Dorothy's love for Toto, her only friend in the real—too real, sometimes, courtesy of Miss Gulch—gray world.

We may never be fortunate enough to travel down a yellow brick road with a real Scarecrow or Tin Man or Cowardly Lion, but those lucky of us have had or do have our Totos. When we stroke and hold our own current four-legged friends, we think of all the dogs that came before. And we think of Toto.

It was mid-afternoon when I found myself sitting in my car on Riverside Drive with that metal box in my hands. A box that contained something every bit as incredible as L. Frank Baum's original story.

For, inside that metal box, was a leather-bound book. A scrapbook.

And on the cover of the book were the words: **I, TOTO**.

Amazingly, what I held in my hands was the scrapbook of a movie star. But not just any movie star. It was a book of memories kept throughout a career by...a tiny dog.

—Willard Carroll
Winter, 2001

ABOVE: My first collectible: a plastic Toto hand puppet contained in a box of Ivory Snow. (Proctor & Gamble, 1965.) Today there are over 20,000 items in my collection. RIGHT: Toto and Prince pose with Risë Stevens in The Chocolate Soldier *(MGM, 1941.)*

I, TOTO

My Scrapbook of Memories

By Toto (a.k.a. Terry)

Many thanks
by Carl Spitz
& Toto, too

My official MGM
studio portrait. It's
how I'd always like
to be remembered —
limber, clear-eyed and
so eager to please.

I AM BORN

Mr. Carl was reading a book to his children the other day — he has a boy and a girl — and I listened in. I don't remember all the details, and it was a long book, and I fell asleep before the end of the second chapter, but I remember it started with the words: "I am born."

I thought that was odd. How can somebody remember when they were born? I certainly don't.

I'd like to start at the beginning — start with my beginning — but I don't really remember much about it. I know I was born in Alta Dena, California, in 1933. And I'm pretty certain that there were more like me — maybe two, maybe three — and I remember that there was a bigger one. Now, of course, I know that the big one was my mom.

I don't really remember what she looked like. I mean, I'm not simple — I know she looked like me. More or less.

I am a purebred, you know.

When I close my eyes and am about to drift off into one of my naps, I can sometimes recall how she smelled. And how she tasted! Nothing has ever smelled or tasted that, well...tasty. Not even Mrs. Carl's cheddar biscuits.

I don't really recall all that much about my first guardians, either. And that's how we prefer to call the people who keep us. We don't like the word "owners." And don't dare say the word "master" in my presence!

One day, not long after I opened my eyes for the first time, these clammy hands picked me up and

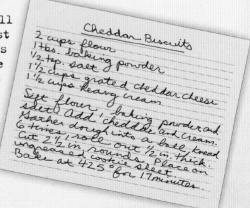

Cheddar Biscuits

2 cups flour
1 tbs. baking powder
1/2 tsp. salt
1 1/2 cups grated cheddar cheese
1 1/2 cups heavy cream

Sift flour, baking powder and salt. Add cheddar and cream. Gather dough into a ball. Knead 6 times. Roll out 1/2 in. thick. Cut 2 1/2 in. rounds. Place on ungreased cookie sheet. Bake at 425° for 17 minutes.

took me away from the big one who smelled and tasted so nice.

I know I cried all the way to my new home in nearby Pasadena. I had to sleep alone on a cement floor next to a noisy, leaky washing machine. My bones ached that first morning when I woke up in those strange surroundings. And I cried again, interspersed with some whimpering and whining, and an occasional yelp.

Pretty soon, I figured out that my guardians — a married couple without any kids — were a bit impatient with me. And, come to think of it, with each other. It got worse and worse. In the way they dealt with me, and with each other.

Primarily, this was because I had another problem.

Oh, dear, I've just begun and already I'm confessing! But I think it's good to be totally honest with my readers. Not that anyone would ever care to read this. I'm really doing this for myself. Why? Because I've had a good life and I've been thinking about it a lot lately and I figured, why not write it down? And, please don't think this immodest of me, but I am a major movie star! Even if I have retired from the silver screen.

Truthfully, I guess I'm sorta embarrassed because, well, my problem involved my, you know, not being able to control my, you know, my wetting.

There, I've said it. And in print, too.

It seems I used to wet everything — rugs, beds, car seats, the occasional lap — you get the picture. My guardians most certainly did.

They tried to cure me. In their own unique way I guess they did their best. Thing is, though, their own unique way involved towering over me, voices raised, and swatting me with a rolled-up newspaper. The yelling and the hitting and the slamming of doors only frightened me and, without fail, well, you guessed it. Another fluid accident.

So one day my guardians tossed me — and I choose my words precisely — tossed me into their car and drove me to the San Fernando Valley.

For those of you who don't know Los Angeles, the Valley is this incredibly beautiful place with rows and rows of orange trees and beautiful ranch houses. The air is crisp and clear and everything smells wonderful. It's paradise on earth!

I found myself in a sort of boarding school for dogs. Cute place. There was a Saint Bernard, a mastiff, a Great Dane, a collie, and almost a dozen other varieties of dogs. And each and every one of them was much bigger than me.

My guardian and my friend, Carl Spitz.

I had to live with a LOT of stress during those early days — I call it my concrete floor period. I assumed I was at this new place to learn something. There was a big sign hanging out front, which read: "Spitz's Hollywood Dog Training School."

Hango, one of my first playmates.

EDITOR'S NOTE: The little girl is Carl Spitz's niece, Hango Dennison, pictured here with Terry in 1933.

19

Note to reader: I'm compelled to explain something here. There's this misguided belief that dogs can't read. That's almost as silly as believing that dogs can't talk! We have a natural aptitude for both. But, just like I had to learn some things, so do humans. And learn this — we most definitely can read. When you lay down all that newspaper for us, what do you think we do with it? Well, of course, we do that, too, but when you're on a sheet of it, doing your duty, you might as well read. <u>The Los Angeles Times</u> was my grammar school. Later, I graduated to <u>Daily Variety</u>. And, furthermore, if we <u>want</u> to talk, we will. We simply have to be motivated. And to have something worth saying.

Mr. Carl and me rehearsing.

INDIVIDUAL CHARACTERISTICS

NO TWO INDIVIDUALS, WHETHER MAN, MOUSE OR DOG, ARE EXACTLY ALIKE. SOME LEARN EASILY...SOME ARE SLOW TO LEARN. THOSE WHICH LEARN QUICKLY, HOWEVER, ARE SOMETIMES NOT AS DEPENDABLE AS OTHER INDIVIDUALS WHICH REQUIRE A LITTLE MORE PATIENCE AND TIME. — Carl Spitz

First day, first hour, this man — Mr. Carl — takes me out of my kennel and starts making all these hand signals and repeating things over and over. I remember thinking, he's sort of amusing. Very animated. And he certainly had patience. It was all very repetitive, but he was so sincere that all I wanted to do was make him happy. So I decided to reward him.

Two days later, I'm rolling around, lying on my back with my paws in the air, playing dead (not my favorite routine), standing up on my hind legs, and barking when requested. Second or third day, Mr. Carl took me inside and introduced me to the family. There's his wife and young son and daughter — and they share Mr. Carl's style. No yelling, no slamming doors, no grouchy attitudes.

The Kennel I call home.
Beats Pasadena any day.

They applaud when I go through my routines. Mr. Carl bristles at the term "tricks." "Tricks are what magicians do," I heard him say once. "Dogs perfect routines."

And there I was, perfecting right and left.

When I finish with my performance, they pet me with such affection. I didn't have too much petting in Pasadena. Maybe they just don't breed petters there.

Well, that day, I was in Mr. Carl's living room, rolling around and ever so excited that they're ever so excited that...well, I have a little accident on the throw rug.

Humans can move so quickly when they want to!

One minute I was in the living room and everybody was all smiles and the next, I was scooped up and placed — placed, not tossed — back in my kennel.

No one was smiling any longer.

And all the other dogs just stared at me and shook their heads in disgust. And then it dawned on me.

You're not supposed to tinkle in the parlor!

So I started barking — just to let Mr. Carl

In the backyard with Prince.
And wasn't he just?

know that I'd figured it out. But he didn't
come back. Not for the longest time. Almost
five minutes.

Yet another note to the reader: To a dog, five minutes away from
you is an eternity. We can read, yes, but a proper sense of time
was omitted from our genetic code. If anyone ever reads this tome
and takes only one thing away from it, this should be it: Never
leave us. Not even for a moment! Of course, we realize you have
to be out of our sight sometimes. But, do us a favor. When you
do, feel guilty about it. Thanks.

Anyway, later that afternoon, all is apparently forgiven. A few days later, and after
much more instruction, I got to go back into
the house. But I'm no dummy. I know this is
a test.
There were all those smiles again. And the
kitchen smelled so wonderful. And I was so
happy and excited and I felt something stir-
ring, something about to happen. But I did my
best to hold it — and I <u>did</u>. I <u>did</u> hold it!
And there were more smiles and more petting
and then even wider smiles and longer petting
moments and a smattering of applause. Life at
that moment was just swell. Just one big darn
heap of swellness.

An aside: A year or so later I hear Mr. Carl tell Mrs. Carl this
joke: There's this dog cowering behind a chair. He turns and speaks
to a cat who is also cowering behind the chair. He says: "Every
time we tear at the sofa, our guardians swat us with a newspaper."
The cat nods and replies: "I've noticed! What a coincidence!"

One day, there was some whispering between
Mr. and Mrs. Carl, during which they gave me
sidelong glances. Again, I'm no dummy and I
quickly realized these mumblings concerned
me. So I gave myself a quick sniff to make
certain I hadn't offended. But everything was
okay down there. One might even say spring-
fresh!

It turns out the people who had brought me to Mr. Carl's — the screamers from Pasadena — hadn't paid the rent on my kennel board. Mr. Carl tried to contact them but their telephone had been disconnected owing to — how did Mr. Carl put it? — "non-payment of the bill."

So, Mr. Carl muttered "deadbeats" under his breath several times and agreed with Mrs. Carl's suggestion that they keep me.

So I found myself with a permanent home. I couldn't have been happier. Way I looked at it, the Pasadena deadbeats had done me a good turn.

A note to the reader: I must explode a myth, which is occasionally perpetrated by non-dog people. We do not just pretend to love you because you feed us! Food is a top priority, yes, but we don't have the innate gift for manipulation that some humans do. After all, we're only dumb animals! And now for a very important aside: We love it when you smile at us. And we try to smile back. We do. Golden retrievers, for some reason, can really pull off this smiling. Although Coralee, one of Mr. Carl's retrievers, confided to me one day that it's just the way their jawbones are constructed. Coralee says it only appears that they're smiling. But she swore me to secrecy. "Let humans believe the smiling routine! It makes 'em feel good. And usually results in larger portions."

Eventually, I began to notice that several of the dogs in Mr. Carl's establishment would sometimes disappear for the entire day. It was revealed to me that a few of my friends were trotted off to places called "studios" and paid handsomely to play pretend all day long! I learned a new word: "movies." Evidently, this is when people dress up and act silly and then other people pay to see them doing it.

The dog that seemed to be pretending the most was Buck. He was this huge St. Bernard. Sorta scary because he was so big. But, come to find out, he was a sweetheart. Very gentle. He would lay down on the ground with his four paws stretched out so he was low enough for me to climb on his back. Then, he'd race around the property with me holding on for dear life. This used to amuse the others. And I had a grand time, too.

Well, about this time, Buck had finished making a movie by the name of <u>Call of the Wild</u>. There was a human in it who I guess was something of a big deal. His name was Clark and female humans responded particularly enthusiastically to the mention of his name.

One day, the humans at Mr. Carl's were all aflutter. Mrs. Carl even had her hair groomed that morning — which she usually only did for funerals.

I soon found out what all the hubbub was about. Someone they called a "studio publicist" was coming with someone named Miss Hopper to take pictures of Buck in his natural surroundings. And this man Clark was coming too!

All these visitors showed up at once. Buck spied Mr. Gable and ran to him. "Hi, there, boy!" Mr. Gable said.

Buck rolled over immediately and did the submissive thing (and Buck hardly ever does the submissive thing!). He's usually what they call dominant or what I'd call "alpha."

The publicist went about "setting up the shot" while Miss Hopper jotted down notes she called "background." Miss Hopper was a gossip columnist, though I didn't know what that meant at the time.

I gathered that something about "not having

Mr. Gable and Buck.

EDITOR'S NOTE: From Call of the Wild, *20th Century Pictures, 1935.*

Buck thought this official fan club portrait made him look ridiculous. I told him, we're paid good money to look ridiculous. Don't grumble. (Personally, I think he looks just swell).

For breakfast Buck eats a quart of milk, 1 egg and a handful of dog biscuits. For dinner Buck eats 4 pounds of beef stew and 2 pounds of cooked vegetables.

film in the camera for the first ten shots" was of some concern to the publicist and Miss Hopper. She used several words I'd never heard before. Even in Pasadena!

Then, just as quickly as he had arrived, Mr. Gable shook hands with everybody and made a move to leave. Without meeting ME!

And so, I barked. And I mean HOWLED!

Everybody turned — man, woman, child, and dog — as if they couldn't believe that such a big sound had come from such a tiny dog. But it did the trick. Mr. Gable, Miss Hopper, and Mr. Spitz headed my way.

Mr. Gable knelt down on the ground so that he was eye-to-eye with me and, gee, did he have nice eyes. He looked at me kindly and said, "Let's get a closer gander at this beauty."

Mr. Carl opened the door to my cage and, well, I was just so darn excited that I flew straight out. Just as I made contact with Mr. Gable's head, I felt something move under me and sail onto the ground. Turns out Mr. Gable had store-bought teeth and they weren't affixed too securely. How was I to know?

Anyway, everybody was scrambling around on all fours — and I don't mean the canines! The Spitz family and Miss Hopper were crawling around looking for Mr. Gable's stray chompers.

Mr. Carl found the teeth and sheepishly handed them back to Mr. Gable who turned away from everybody for a moment and hastily reinstated them. Ever so slowly, Mr. Gable turned back, leaned down, and whispered to me, "Lesson for the day: take care of your teeth." Then he laughed. And laughed and laughed!

Mrs. Spitz picked me up, rubbed the top of my head, and handed me to Mr. Gable who held me next to his face. He smiled again, and rubbed his finger under my chin in a way I adore! And, then, to demonstrate that the feeling was mutual, I gave him a good, long, wet lick.

Mr. Gable handed me back to Mrs. Spitz, got into his car, and drove away. My first encounter with a movie star!

Buck's playing pretend. What he's really pretending is that he doesn't know how silly this looks. Trust me, he does.

EDITOR'S NOTE: From the 1938 MGM movie Hold That Kiss. *From left to right: Dennis O'Keefe, Buck, Maureen O'Sullivan.*

Miss Hopper and Mr. Carl. Miss Hopper was a frequent visitor to the kennel. She was always asking Mr. Carl for the "inside scoop" on the movies us dogs were making. Mr. Carl really liked her though Mrs. Carl often joked about those funny hats Miss Hopper wore. Personally, I'm fond of anybody with style.

I spent that evening on Mrs. Spitz's lap in the living room as the family told the Clark story over and over again. I fell asleep as she gently stroked me, and I woke up next morning at the foot of the Spitz's bed. It was the first time I'd spent an entire night inside a house proper (the Pasadena laundry room didn't count).

Just before I woke up, I dreamed of another morning when I slept beside my mother. In the dream I had a brother and a sister and even though my eyes weren't open yet, I saw my mother's face. And she was looking down at me and smiling. She was! Really smiling. Not just a golden retriever smile. And she was proud. She was! You don't make up a dream. As I awoke, I smelled freshly baked cheddar biscuits. Mrs. Spitz gave me an extra one that day. Sometimes, you just can't improve on a morning.

The happy feeling was an omen. A good one. The very next day, Mr. Carl carried me to his car.

At first, I was a little worried as we drove away. I stood up on the front seat with

my paws on the top and gazed back at the kennel and my friends. I emitted a brief series
of whines because I had this terrible fear.
Was I going away for good? Or for bad? My
worst case scenario: Mr. Carl was taking me
back to Pasadena!

After what seemed an eternity, we
drove through the gates of this impos-
ing place called Fox. A studio. A
movie studio! I knew what that was. I
was squatting on Variety by this time!

Mr. Carl was given this little slip
of paper by this guy named "Security"
who was dressed up in some sort of
costume that didn't fit too well. Mr.
Carl was told to leave the paper on
the dashboard. I guessed that this
paper proved that Mr. Carl's rabies
shots were up-to-date. He had my
papers with him in his jacket pock-
et. And I knew all my shots were
current.

We parked. Mr. Carl put me on a
leash, and we walked to this big,
big room. Even though it was hot
outside that day, inside it was
freezing.

*EDITOR'S NOTE: Shirley Temple
and Buck, Spanish trading
card, 1934.*

I was most eager to meet my co-
stars and start working in the movie.

Mr. Carl was approached by a burly man who
didn't smile and who told him to take a seat
with the others.

Others!?

We were shown into another, even colder,
room with seven — count 'em - seven! — cairn
terriers and their respective guardians. And
what a rowdy bunch! Yapping and scratching and
squealing and growling and emitting these
foul smells. One little cur produced a series
of high notes which would have made Kate
Smith envious. I lay down and put my paws over
my ears.

And then, as if the sound emanating from
her-highness-with-the-tonsils wasn't excruci-
ating enough, one mangy candidate scurried
over to the middle of that room and — well,
right there on the rug! And we're not talking wee-wee! As if that wasn't enough, the
little guy stepped in it and left tracks
everywhere. I closed my eyes and shook my
head. Amateurs!

One by one — hopping with expectation — the
dogs were led into a small room by their
guardians where they each stayed exactly
three minutes. And one by one they came out
— their muzzles drawn, their tails between
their legs. And those were the trainers! The
dogs looked even more depressed.

I looked up at Mr. Carl and thought, if
this is the movie business you can have it!

So I started to shiver — just a little —
and Mr. Carl gave me a little pat on the head
and said "Good girl" in a soft, soothing
voice. I stopped shivering.

An immensely important note to the reader: Sometimes all it takes
to make the worry go away is a little pat on the head and a
"Good girl." Or, "Good boy." Depending.

We were the last to go in through that door.
But I had renewed confidence.

The door closed behind us with a loud thud,
like a prison gate slamming for all eternity.
Seated at a long table were three very seri-
ous-looking men. The entire time we were
there, they never smiled or showed any enthusiasm whatsoever. These must be those guys
called "studio executives" I'd read about.

"Let's see what the little mutt can do,"
says one guy.

Mr. Carl gives me a look which says, don't
worry about the name-calling, and just go into
my dance. So, I roll over. Expertly.

No response from the three suits.

I leap over the leash.
No response.
I play dead.
No response.
I bark on command.
No response.
I growl on command (this took very little prompting from Mr. Carl.)

Again no response. They just stared.

After I had exhausted my repertoire — and it's fairly extensive at this point — the three guys looked at each other and shrugged. They shrugged!

So I'm thinking: "Mr. Carl, can I bite them? Please, Mr. Carl, let me bite them! Please! Please! Please!"

But I held my tongue. Literally.

Finally one dolt broke the silence: "I guess she's...okay."

I make a move towards him, but Mr. Carl holds me back.

A second dullard chimes in: "Sorta on the runty side."

The third nitwit sighs like he's been working hard and he says: "I can't tell one from the other."

The first guy says: "Let's see what Shirley thinks."

And the three men all nodded in unison — like those bobbing-head statues you see on the dashboards of some cars. One of them pressed a button on a box on the desk.

I backed away from them and bumped into Mr. Carl, who looked down and gave me a little nod.

Another note to the reader: Sometimes a little nod at just the right moment speaks volumes.

I calmed down. The first guy spoke into the box: "Could you please see if Miss Temple is available?"

A few minutes later we were escorted across

Shirley's bungalow on the Fox lot.

the studio lot. We went into yet another building called a bungalow. "Bungalow" sounds like an exotic dance or something, but it's just a fancy name for a small house.

There was a tiny room just inside the door with nothing on the wall and a kinda weird-looking woman who was sitting behind a desk reading a racing form.

She stood when she saw us and said, "Right this way."

We were shown through yet another doorway into a room that was pink and frilly. Toys were everywhere. Trains. A wagon. A scooter. A little tea set at a tiny table. And dolls! Whoever lived there was evidently partial to one doll in particular. On the shelves were 38 (I counted them later) dolls.

And although each of the dolls was wearing a different outfit, they were all the same. The same face, the same eyes, the same dimple, the same golden curls, the same knickers.

Suddenly, a side door opened and in walked a little girl — a little girl who was made-up to look <u>exactly</u> like those dolls. Same

Doesn't Shirley look just like her doll?

face, eyes, golden curls, same
knickers, even the same dimple
in the cheek.

Most importantly, though, the
real little girl had a big,
friendly, infectious smile.
She took one look at me and
said: "Oh, she's so cute!"

I'd been about to say
the same thing about her.

I could tell right off
she was a dog person. She
fell to her knees and
scooped me up and kissed me
on the nose. I responded by
licking her cheek — at first
lightly and a bit dryly.
Just to test the waters, see
if she liked it.

And she did like it! She
giggled and kissed me again.
Licks, kisses. Kisses, licks. This exchange
went back-and-forth for quite some time — not
that either one of us was complaining — until
I looked over her shoulder and saw another
dog. A Pomeranian.

"Let me guess," I remember thinking. "My
competition. It's between me and this frilly
mutt."

Shirley looks at me and says: "I think
she's adorable. Let's see how Ching-Ching
feels."

Shirley stood up and backed away. I took a
look at Ching-Ching and then at Mr. Carl. He
gave me another little head nod and I walked
slowly over to the Pomeranian.

I realized that she wasn't a candidate for
the role in the movie but some sort of con-

sultant to Shirley. I'd better do my best
sweetness number on this compadre, I thought.

There was a semi-awkward standoff between
Ching-Ching and me for a moment. The doggie
appeared very noncommittal.

And then I thought, what have I got to
lose? So, I rolled over on my back with my
feet sticking straight up in the air. This
seemed to do the trick with Ching-Ching. There
was a little mutual sniffing, and then we
started running around the room, taking turns
chasing the other, jumping on the furniture,
tumbling about. All in all, a swell playtime.

Then reality intruded. Everything came to
a screeching halt when the three
guys from the audition appeared in
the doorway. (I would discover
later that, whenever they arrive,
all the fun stops.) Mr. Carl looked
glum. Ching-Ching lost her joie de
vivre. Even Shirley's dimple
seemed to disappear. Really!

Shirley Temple

Finally, though, it was little
Shirley who broke the silence. She
picked me up, handed me back to
Mr. Carl, scooped up Ching-Ching,
and skipped to the door. Without
turning back to face the executives she said, with girlish
enthusiasm and absolute decisive-
ness, "She's hired!"

And that was it!

The Fox picture was called
Bright Eyes, and I soon learned Shirley
got whatever she wanted. She had "director
approval," which, evidently, every star wanted but hardly anyone ever got. That means she
can say who is hired to tell her what to do
on the set but, since she's the one who did
the hiring, she's really the boss. Shirley
knew how to take charge but, at the same time,
she knew how to have fun. Some people make it

I loved working with Shirley Temple on <u>Bright Eyes</u> even though, between takes, we had to pose for endless publicity shots. Buck said he'd NEVER allow himself to be harnessed like a work horse but there was nothing I wouldn't do for Shirley. Like the rest of America, I was a sucker for those curls and dimples.

Here I am with Shirley and James Dunn in <u>Bright Eyes</u>. I'd work with Mr. Dunn again, six years later, in <u>Son of the Navy</u>. Both of us would like to forget that picture, but we'll always remember this one with affection.

look hard. Shirley made it look easy.

There's a lot that happens during "pre-production" — that's a period of time before the cameras actually roll — particularly when it comes to us actors.

To prepare for her part in the picture, Shirley had her hair cut and re-curled and had endless wardrobe fittings and makeup tests.

I had a flea bath, a toenail trim, and an enema.

I played the character of "Rags" and it was a <u>major</u> role. I counted my barks in the script, and I had almost as many lines as Shirley did!

It takes time and care to make a movie. On the set of <u>Bright Eyes</u> there was a lot of waiting around. I used the downtime to

Shirley Temple

perfect my routines — running, jumping, tug-
ging-the-heartstrings (the last one came nat-
urally to me.) And I took a lot of naps.

Note to reader: Yes, it's true! Dogs do take a lot of naps. On the
average about 65 a day. Being a pet is hard work. Let alone
being an actor!

Shirley had a stand-in. That was a little
girl who looked just like her — same size,
same height, wore the same costumes and everything. (She didn't have a dimple, though, and
her hair always looked wilted.)

The stand-in would wait under the hot
lights while everybody moved around her getting everything just right for when Shirley
returned. Then the stand-in would go away, and
Shirley would turn on the magic.

Between takes during
the filming of Bright
Eyes. That's Shirley
and her stand-in
(Shirley's on the left).

I remember hoping that maybe, someday, I'd have my very own stand-in.

I never slept more soundly at night
than during a movie shoot. Mind you,
in the morning, there was
nothing on my mind except
making a tiny deposit in the
bushes behind the kennels
or, better yet, on yester-
day's Variety. When you're
in the biz you have to keep
up on things.

I was staying inside the
Spitz's house all the time
by then in my own little
basket under the kitchen
sink. I liked that spot
because I could see everyone coming and going. The

EDITOR'S NOTE: Bright Eyes *was also
the first substantial film role for
actress Jane Withers who went on to
be the second-highest-paid child star
of the decade, after Shirley Temple.*

Shirley always gave her fellow actors tremendous support, even when she was acting "angry." I worked hard to bring the same emotion to my face. I was so fortunate in my career to learn my craft from the best in the business.

door was always open, and I could go out and come back whenever I pleased.

The other dogs seemed very happy for me.

One day towards the end of shooting Bright Eyes, I experienced one of those mysterious, spine-chilling moments that haunt you afterwards. Haunt you in a good way.

During lunch breaks, Shirley and Ching-Ching had me as their guest. I had my own little bowl with "Terry" written on it. (It had two of those backwards 'R' letters on it. I hate that. How's a kid to learn when somebody plays cute with the alphabet?)

One lunchtime, after Shirley had finished off three bowls of alphabet soup, she started reading a book. Shirley really enjoyed that book because she smiled at something on every page and laughed sometimes, too.

I couldn't see the title — Shirley's hand covered it — but on the cover was a picture of a cute little girl walking between two of the strangest creatures you ever saw. One of them looked like a burlap bag with eyes painted on it and the other like tin cans strung together without their labels. What really caught my eye was a tiny dog on the bottom of the cover. It wasn't my identical breed, though there were some similarities. The illustrator had taken some liberties; the dog looked like a cairn crossed with a dachshund. (I shudder at the thought!)

I remember wondering what happened to that little dog. You know, in the story. Little did I know then that that book would change my life forever.

When we finished shooting Bright Eyes, they had this little celebration called a wrap party. That's where everybody gets together and drinks a great deal.

It seems that crying was standard behavior at wrap par-

EDITOR'S NOTE: Illustrations by W. W. Denslow from the first edition of The Wonderful Wizard of Oz, 1900.

ties. Shirley gave me a good long hug, and I have to tell you I whimpered a bit. I was going to miss her. Everybody was bawling and saying that they loved everybody else and they all swore to keep in touch. Sounded great, although I never crossed paths with any of the crew again.

I guess that's the movie business.

I made another movie that year at another studio — a Paramount picture called Ready for Love. I auditioned for that role, too. I'd swear the same three guys who interviewed me at Fox were the ones I met at Paramount.

I don't remember too much about Ready for Love. Except that the food wasn't as good at Paramount and there was no dish with my name on it. The thing that remained unchanged from my Fox days was the pre-production routine — flea bath, toenail trim, enema.

The next year rolled around awfully fast and there I was at another studio — this time United Artists for a picture called Dark Angel.

And, boy! do those three guys in suits get around! Same clothes, same expressions, same "I don't want to say 'yes,' and I don't want to say 'no'" routine.

I worked with an actor called Frederic March in that picture. He liked the ladies. He was more partial to the two-legged variety, but he occasionally threw a squeeze my way. The major two-legged lady was Merle Oberon. Sort of a funny name — sounded to me like she made it up or something — but, boy, was she pretty!

Merle was a little standoffish, though. Couldn't be bothered with the peons, if you catch my drift. And when you're a dog, well, some people treat you like they wouldn't treat a dog!

I didn't have too big a part in Dark Angel, and the story really wasn't to my liking. Too soapy! And one of the characters went off to

something called "the war," and there were all
sorts of loud noises and these huge things
that looked like fans called "wind machines."
I don't like loud noises. And I particularly
don't like wind machines. I remember thinking
that I would make a condition of my further
employment: no movies with loud noises or wind
machines.

Well, another year came and went, and I found
myself at yet another studio auditioning for
yet another three suits. By this time, though,
I was seasoned. I just walked in there, strut-
ted my stuff, gave them a "hire-me-or-don't-
hire-me-there-are-other-studios-in-this-town"
look, turned tail, and departed. I learned that
when you appear as if you could care less about
a job, you're suddenly irresistible.

I got the job and was glad I did!

I worked with a man named Spencer Tracy and
the picture was called Fury. Mr. Tracy made
everything look easier than even Shirley had.
You could hardly tell he was acting at all!
I learned a lot of technique from Spence (his
friends call him Spence). All about doing not
very much to get a big effect.

The director, Mr. Lang, was a little scary
at first. He wore this big monocle and everyone seemed very intimidated by him. Mr. Lang
and Mr. Carl got along great, though, because
it turned out they were both from Germany.
They could speak in that tongue. They got sad
when they were together sometimes, though.

From what I could gather, they both missed
their homeland, but something was going on
there that made it difficult to go back, even
if they wanted to.

Sometimes they forgot themselves and gave
me direction in German. I had no idea what
they were saying, of course. I know a little
French, and my Italian is passable — but
German? Too guttural! Couldn't make head nor
tails of it.

Me and Spence in <u>Fury</u>. I remember being really scared when the jail door slammed and Spence clutched me to him. Then I realized Spence was only acting. (My character's name in this movie was 'Rainbow'. Now was that an omen or what?)

I was back at Paramount for <u>The Buccaneer</u>. On this picture, the three suits made no pretence of who was in charge. That Cecil B. DeMille could do anything! He's what they call a hyphenate. That's somebody who gets paid a lot more because they have their name on the screen credits more times than anybody else.

He carried this big megaphone, which he really didn't need. My former guardians could have heard him bossing everybody around all the way out in Pasadena.

<u>The Buccaneer</u> was my first costume picture. And the costumes were lovely. I kept watching as everyone went from fitting to fitting — actors going into the dressing rooms wearing the latest street fashions and then coming out looking like pirates.

I kept waiting for my fitting but had to settle for a flea bath, a nail trim, and an enema.

I hesitate to mention my next picture. It's what Mr. Carl referred to as a "B movie." They were being kind if you ask me! I'd give it a "G." But Mr. Carl says you can't go any lower than an "F." Well, then,

Spence has just given me the best actor-to-actor advice I ever received. "Terry," he said, "learn your lines, don't bump into the furniture, and don't pee on anything you eat." He was a genius!

All I kept thinking
during this scene was,
"My, what a big gun
you've got there!"

they never saw <u>Barefoot Boy</u>! It was shot on
what was called <u>Poverty Row</u> and, let me tell
you, that was an accurate location because the
picture was strictly from hunger.

The only refreshing thing was that there
weren't the customary three suits at the audition. Seems they could only afford one suit.
And what a suit that guy wore! It didn't look
like it had been pressed since Buck was a pup
and, to top it off, he wore the same one every
day. If you ask me, he's the one who needed
the flea bath, nail trim and, well...I'll stop
there.

Come to find out, though, that Mr. Tatty
ran the studio!

Anyway, they were so cheap at Monogram that
they didn't even bother to come up with a name
for my character. "Call it
'Terry!'" the studio boss said.
"That's its name, ain't it?"

I gave him a very mean look
that warned, "Watch who you're
calling <u>it</u>, buddy!"
That schlub worked us so hard
— hour after hour with no
breaks just to get the film "in

I'm just a blur here because
Franciska got a little carried
away. I had to say, "I'm
not quite ready for my
close-up Mr. DeMille!"

*EDITOR'S NOTE: Production
stills from* The Buccaneer, *
Paramount, 1938.*

the can." They even used one of those rusty cans to put my grub in. Boy, did I miss Shirley. And Fox. And Paramount. I even missed those three guys I met everywhere!

After one particularly grueling day, the studio boss came down and told us to pick up the pace.

Pick up the pace!? If we were working any faster, we'd have the movie in theaters by the weekend.

So this studio boss stands there and yells and yells. And he says, "I want the picture in theaters by the weekend."

Mr. Carl and I started to chuckle. Maybe Mr. Crabby has a sense of humor, after all, I thought.

But he wasn't kidding.

Well, this news did not go over well with the crew, and it went down particularly NOT well with Mr. Carl. The boss walked over to the center of the soundstage and bellowed: "Finish this movie by Saturday, or you're all through! I'm serious!"

Mr. Carl couldn't take this abuse any longer, and he strode right up to that guy and said: "If you're so serious then why are you wearing that suit?"

The crew had their hands poised to applaud Mr. Carl but backed down when they saw the look on the boss's face.

Later that day, Mr. Carl and I were told by the "production manager" — he does all the jobs on the set that are beneath everybody else — that we didn't need to return to the set the next day. Fine by me. We had finished my part in the movie anyway.

As we drove home, Mr. Carl was not the least bit depressed because we'd been fired. He said something about "taking the bitter with the sour." I nodded in agreement.

When we got home that night, there was some

For my money, this is the only memorable moment from most Monogram Pictures— certainly the two I made there!

major excitement in the Spitz household.
Turns out there had been a call from one of
the three suits at MGM. Mr. Carl and I were
being summoned to some producer's office the
very next day to discuss a picture.

Truth be told, I would have liked some time
off, but when it's your day in the sun, you
have to strike while the iron is hot.

The next day, I was taken to MGM where I
had worked on Fury. It was a nice place. There
was lots of grass, and there was a favorite
bush of mine behind which I always ducked on
my way to auditions.

Note to the reader: There is something I want to get straight for
the record. Later in my career, some writer accused me — in
print, mind you! — of raising my leg to her after I had expressed
displeasure over an article about me in Modern Screen. Lies, lies, lies!
As anyone with half a brain knows, boy dogs raise their legs. Lady
dogs squat. And that's what I did with that hack from Modern
Screen. All over her pumps. Raise my leg, indeed!

Meanwhile, back at MGM, we were shown into
the producer's office — bypassing the three
suits. This guy must be important! And, come
to find out, Mr. LeRoy's the major mucky-muck
on this new movie that's about to
start shooting.

In his office, even before
he made a move to pull a book
off the shelf, this little
chill ran up and down my
spine. Mr. LeRoy handed Mr.
Carl the book. And this is
where it gets weird! Good
weird. But weird.

It was the same book that
Shirley was reading back at
Fox all that time ago. The
one with the funny characters on
the cover. And the little dog. Could it be?
Did they want me to play that little dog?

Well, turns out the roles in this movie were what they call "coveted." Now I've never really coveted anything — okay steak-and-kidney pie, occasionally — but not something as silly as a film role.

The producer bandied about all these names. A man named Buddy was going to play the Tin Man (that's the guy who looks like he's made of soup cans). And someone named Ray was going to be the Scarecrow, the burlap sack with eyes. A guy named Bert had been hired to play some sort of lion who's a big sissy. There wasn't a lion on the book cover so I figured maybe he was added for the movie. They often do that, you know.

Out in front with all of my best friends from The Wizard of Oz. (Well, not all. Those studio meanies wouldn't let Maggie join the fun).

It turns out the girl's name is Dorothy. According to Mr. LeRoy, my Shirley wanted to play the role. Then he launched into this very confusing story about "loan-outs," "trading favors," "other candidates" — well, it was way over my head. The gist was that all along he'd wanted an MGM contract player for the part. Apparently, once Mr. LeRoy sets his mind on something, he gets it.

"Contract player" — that phrase is music to my ears. That means they pay you for just sitting around — whether you work or not. Now, that's making it big time. I hope I am in that position someday. And the first rule I'll lay down under my new contract will be: ENOUGH ALREADY WITH THE ENEMAS!

I didn't get the full name of the actress who was to play Dorothy. Only her first name: Judy. Mr. LeRoy called everybody by his or her first names, but everybody had to call him "Mr. LeRoy." I guess that's <u>really</u> making it.

All I could think was, "I hope Judy's as nice as Shirley."

In all the fuss, I forgot why I was there. To audition. But Mr. LeRoy just looked down at me, then at the dog on the cover of the book and said: "She's the one! Looks just like the dog on the cover."

Now, neither Mr. Carl nor myself was going to argue and say that the dog on the cover of the book was a genetic mutation of terrifying

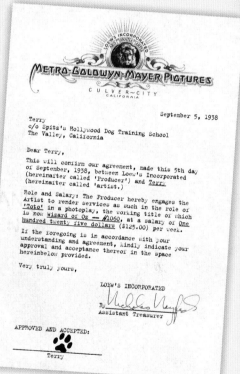

September 5, 1938

Terry
c/o Spitz's Hollywood Dog Training School
The Valley, California

Dear Terry,

This will confirm our agreement, made this 5th day of September, 1938, between Loew's Incorporated (hereinafter called 'Producer') and Terry (hereinafter called 'artist.)

Role and Salary: The Producer hereby engages the Artist to render services as such in the role of 'Toto' in a photoplay, the working title of which is now <u>Wizard of Oz — #1060</u>, at a salary of <u>One hundred twenty five dollars</u> ($125.00) per week.

If the foregoing is in accordance with your understanding and agreement, kindly indicate your approval and acceptance thereof in the space hereinbelow provided.

Very truly yours,

LOEW'S INCORPORATED

By
Assistant Treasurer

APPROVED AND ACCEPTED:

Terry

proportions — and certainly no breed I would call my own — but, what-the-hey, I had the job!

I don't have to be a mutation to play one. I'm an actor.

Well, evidently, this opus was going to be some picture because Mr. Carl had to work me something fierce to get me ready. I had to learn all sorts of new stuff, and Mr. Carl broke it to me gently: "Now, Terry, there may be a wind machine or two in this picture."

Bring 'em on! I'm a veteran.

Evidently <u>The Wizard of Oz</u> is some sort of classic and Toto — that's the character I play — is one of literature's most famous dogs. I vowed that day that I was gonna play the heck outta her. And do literature proud.

Oh, and here's the best part — I found out later that day that the movie was gonna be in TECHNICOLOR!

I had never been in color before. Well, you know what I mean by that. I, personally, <u>am</u> in color if you

This was my first public appearance, two years before I would achieve my biggest success.

EDITOR'S NOTE: Makeup-test still of Gale Sondegaard in Witch #2 makeup. Sondegaard was originally cast as the Wicked Witch of the West in The Wizard of Oz, later replaced by Margaret Hamilton. Sondegaard was rejected because she was "too beautiful."

MISS SONDERGARD WITCH #2 MAKE UP

meet me on the street (say "Hi!" if that happens), but I'd only been black-and-white on the big screen. I had been told that I photographed well in black-and-white but wait until they see me in color.

So we got a copy of the script to take home with us — well at least a version of the script. There are these dates called "revisions" all over the cover of the thing! They don't seem able to make up their minds about certain story points. Characters come and go. Lines of dialogue are crossed out. Scenes are changed. All those writers and nobody can come to an agreement.

Well, turns out, that was just the beginning. Over the next few days, one script after another was delivered to Mr. Carl. He just put them on the stack with the others beside the fireplace. "We'll wait for the one that says 'final shooting script.' No sense you learning something that won't be in the picture."

There was one thing, though, that remained constant in each and every draft — Dorothy and Toto. No matter how many writers take a stab at the movie, Dorothy and Toto remain.

And the closer we got to production, the more I realized — and I don't mean this to sound full of myself — but this Wizard of Oz story? IT'S ALL ABOUT ME!!! I have the closest relationship of anyone to Dorothy. I'm why she runs away from home. And why she does all sorts of things to save me from something called the Wicked Witch. I'M IN ALMOST EVERY SCENE IN THE BLESSED PICTURE!!!

If I'd have known where to find my mother or father, I'd have tracked them down to let them know their kid done good.

First official day of pre-production, Mr. Carl took me to the studio. They gave me the flea bath and the nail trim and this time — they skipped the enema!

I'm gonna love this picture!

So, just like always, every-body was running around with wardrobe fittings and make-up tests. And the make-up on this one! You had to see it to believe it. That guy Bert I told you about? He went into a wardrobe trailer looking all street-normal and came out with whiskers and a big fur coat, roaring like a real ol' lion.

And there was a woman called Maggie who was going to play a dual role. (Later on I found out almost everybody except Judy and I were playing dual roles. I wondered if you got paid twice when you played two roles.)

Anyway, this Maggie person was-n't exactly a looker, but boy was she sweet! And gentle. A real dog person. She walked right over to me that first day, picked me up, held me to her face, and let me lick her. My kind of lady. Maggie handed me back ever so carefully to Mr. Carl and swept into the makeup and wardrobe department.

EDITOR'S NOTE: Toto on stage and screen: Mervyn LeRoy initially envisioned having Toto played by an actor in costume. Indeed, early stage and film adaptations had a recurring problem of how to deal with Toto. The successful 1902 stage production eliminated the dog altogether. Instead, Dorothy went to Oz with Imogene, her cow (an actor in costume.) The Wonderful Wizard of Oz, a 1910 one-reel silent film adaptation produced by film pioneer William Selig, started with a cairn terrier who was then 'transformed' by Glinda into a 'real protector,' an actor in costume, who dwarfed the actress playing Dorothy. The 1925 Larry Semon vehicle also left out the dog. Prior to the MGM film, only one adaptation, the 1933 Ted Esebaugh animated short, portrayed Dorothy with her dog, Toto, as a partner in the complete journey. FROM TOP: Candy box showing Dorothy and Imogene the cow, circa 1903. The Wonderful Wizard of Oz/Selig, 1910. Toto is to the left of the Tin Man. Frames from the Ted Eschbaugh adaptation, 1933.

                        Dorothy
I'm frightened, I'm frightened, Auntie Em -
I'm frightened!

                      Auntie Em
Dorothy - Dorothy - where are you? It's me --
it's Auntie Em. We're trying to find you! Where
are you?

                        Dorothy
I - I'm here in Oz, Auntie Em! I'm locked up in
the Witch's castle .. and I'm trying to get home
to you, Auntie Em! Oh, Auntie Em, don't go away!
I'm frightened! Come back! Come back!

                       Miss Gulch
Auntie Em - Auntie Em - come back! I'll give
you Auntie Em, my pretty! (laughs)

CU of the Hour Glass - sand running rapidly through
to lower half -

                    LAP DISSOLVE TO:

ELS - Ext. Rocks - Toto making his way down
to the bottom - She barks -

                    LAP DISSOLVE TO:

MLS - Toto running forward through forest -
exits out to left, f.g. barking -

MLS - Toto enters from right - CAMERA PANS him
left as he runs through the forest, barking -

MS - Ext. Haunted Forest - Zeke and Hickory are
working on Hunk as they put him back together -
Hickory hears Toto barking o.s - points off to
right -

                       Hickory
Look! There's ...

LS - Toto running forward through forest - CAMERA
PANS him left to Hickory, Zeke and Hunk -
                     Hickory o.s.
...Toto! Where'd he come from?

CU - Toto barks at the three o.s. in f.g. -

CS - Zeke, Hunk and Hickory - Hunk reacts, speaks
to the others -
                        Hunk
Why, don't you see? He's come to take us...

MLS - Zeke, Hunk and Hickory react, rise - Toto
barks, leads them as they run down trail to right
b.g. = CAMERA PANS with them -

I have six lines in this scene! And I'm gonna make the most of them.

For the next two hours, Mr. Carl and I trained so that I could sit on the narrow, cold metal seat of some cockamamie farm contraption. I was supposed to look enraptured for some song that's going to be sung to me. When I felt that cold steel on my little rump all I could think was, "That had better be some song!"

Anyway, just as we'd finished for the day, I hear Mr. Carl say: "Here comes Maggie again!"

So I was all excited — Maggie was such a dear to me earlier — when out of the makeup room comes this, well, I don't know how to describe it! This thing was all green and black and evil-looking with a crooked nose and a chin that hung down to her chest. Then she made this cackling sound that frightened me so much I forgot everything I'd been taught. And I mean everything! Yep, right there on the sound stage floor, I had a major accident. Major!

Perhaps I should've had that enema after all.

Fortunately, nobody seemed angry, least of all Maggie. She picked me up and explained to me that she was the same ol' Maggie and that I should get used to people going into rooms looking one way and coming out looking another.

That's what they call the magic of movies.

Those stagehands were quick! I glanced behind me and my mess had been whisked away. Like magic. I guess a movie star can do anything anywhere and somebody else cleans it up. It's a wonderful business.

And to think I ever thought Maggie was scary!!

If you think Jack looks funny from the front you shoulda seen him from my perspective.

Judy and me in our first photo shoot together.

Judy's not really scolding me.
It's called acting.

I'm down here.
Behind this pitiful
excuse for a
prop tree.

Your command is my wish.
Down? I can do down.

Up? I can do up.

Don't be sad, Judy.
Look what I can do!

We were just about to leave after that long
first day when Mr. LeRoy came to Mr. Carl and
said: "I think it's time Terry met Judy."

I was so very excited to meet the little
girl who was going to play Dorothy. We went
into a very nice dressing room. There was a
girl sitting in a chair reading a book — my,
my these movie people like to read!

I trotted in — a bit apprehensive but trying to be suave — and the girl raised her head
and said: "Hello, I'm Judy!"

Now, the girl who walked over to me was a
bit older than I had pictured the character —
certainly older than the girl on the front of
the book but, golly, she was lovely! Not beautiful in that Merle Oberon way but so, so
pretty. Judy had these delicate freckles and
soft, fragile eyes and when she spoke — well,
it was as if she was singing. And she wasn't
the least bit standoffish. Matter of fact, she
was just like any little girl — only more so.

And, later, when we got around to shooting the scene where she sings to me? Well, all that time Mr. Carl was teaching me to look enraptured, heck, it was a waste of time. Just sitting across from her, even while freezing one's little rear on the icy metal, you wouldn't have to give a performance at all. No acting required.

The first couple of weeks on the shoot were not a lot of laughs. No one seemed particularly happy with the director, Mr. Thorpe. There was a lot of whispering and many late-night meetings. Rumors were flying.

I did everything okay, I thought, but sometimes I would have liked another take or two. Particularly when Dorothy and I first meet the Scarecrow. I was supposed to look at him and bark and, I'm not certain about this, but I think I looked into the camera. And you just do not do that! (Little did I know at the time, all of us would have another chance to do the entire scene over).

During the first take of this scene, I tried to bark along with the tune "We're Off To See The Wizard," but the director wasn't too keen on my improvisation. He gave me the best director-to-actor advice I ever received: "Don't just say something. Stand there!"

I suppose us actors are never satisfied. I wanted Mr. Carl to take me to the rushes (the film we shot the day before) but he said there was a lot of what they call "tension on the set."

All through this tension, though, Judy just plugs along. And so I decided to take a leaf from her book. I did the work best I could and ignored the politics.

Two weeks into the production and the politics reared their head so loudly that they couldn't be ignored. We were told we were shutting down for a time. Seems Mr. Thorpe was going to be replaced by Mr. Fleming, but first Mr. Cukor was going to do some "consulting." That's another word for directing but without the credit.

I remember thinking, "My, directors come and go so quickly here!"

So, Mr. Carl and I headed home and waited. We were called back a week or so later, and I was so happy to see Judy again.

In her new Cukor-approved Dorothy get-up, she looked a bit different. Good different, but different. Her hair was styled more becomingly and her gingham apron was better tailored. Actually, she looked darn perfect. I guess Mr. Cukor knows his way around women.

Now, Maggie, knowing I could get a little frightened and sensing a fellow actor's unease, pulled me aside one day to prepare me for something called "Winkies." I'm thinking, "Winkies" sound sorta okay to me.

herself. As the four actors held on to each other and tried to dance, Toto dodged back and forth behind them and stayed in for a perfect scene.

The hardest thing this little dog ever had to do was during the drawbridge scene in *The Wizard of Oz*, when she was chased by the huge Winkie guards of the Wicked Witch. Toto had to come running out of the castle and try to cross the drawbridge. She had almost reached the middle when the drawbridge was pulled straight up. The only safety Toto had was by clutching the edge of the bridge with her little paws and balancing herself thirty feet in the air. One of a dog's greatest fears is the fear of falling, so it took a great deal of courage to follow her master's orders that time.

Once, in a movie scene, Toto's action called

For once they got every detail of the story right! Don't you think these Winkies are scary?

EDITOR'S NOTE: Clipping from American Girl Magazine, *March, 1940.*

Not scary at all. Has a pleasant ring to it — sorta like "Munchkins" and we know what sweethearts they are.

Well, nothing anybody could have told me would have prepared me for the "Winkies." Sweethearts they ain't! They made the Wicked Witch of the West look like Deanna Durbin.

One day we were shooting and there were dozens of these costumed horrors marching around looking menacing. And this lumbering brute, who never watched where he was going, marched right past me and stepped on my paw.

Now, that Winkie liked his grub, and he must have weighed about a thousand pounds. When he stepped on my foot I squealed. And I mean SQUEALED!

Mr. Carl came running over. The director, Mr. Fleming this week, came running over. Everybody and their sainted aunt came running over. But I was so terrified and in pain that all I could do was squeal and think to myself, I wanna go home!

And they sent me home.

Evidently, Judy had a word with someone called Louie in the front office and told him in no uncertain terms that I needed a rest. I couldn't have agreed with her more!

I was so happy to be off that set and away from those darn Winkies! I crawled into my little basket under the sink and licked my bandaged paw. All I wanted to do was sleep away the pain and the memory of those Winkies.

I'm a hanger!

Well, I was about to nod off when I woke with a start. What if they replace me? What if they reshoot my scenes with some other little dog!?

I unwrapped the bandage, gave the paw a good lick, raced into Mr. and Mrs. Carl's room, and jumped up on their bed.

EDITOR'S NOTE: One of a series of eight hangers manufactured by Barney Stempler & Sons, 1939.

This was such a happy day. We had just finished shooting the Munchkinland scenes. That's Mr. LeRoy standing to the left of Judy (your left, not Judy's) and Mr. Fleming is holding me. The Munchkins were a fun lot. I was looking at Mr. Carl who was giving me the biggest smile! (Probably because he was thinking how much more money I was making than the little people). I smiled right back at him.

I think Mr. Carl may have been looking forward to a few days away from Oz himself, but this was my career! I tugged and tugged at him until finally he said, "I get it. You're ready to go back to work!"

I barked an affirmative.

Next day, we went back to work.

I trotted onto that set all happy-like. They were setting up the scene where we first arrive at the Emerald City. And, there, at the far end of the soundstage, standing in front of the gates, ready for the first shot of the day, were all my friends. There was Judy, and Ray, and Jack, and a cute little dog, and Bert and... A CUTE LITTLE DOG!?!?!?!?!?!?!?!?

Well, I just sorta lost it. One day — not even — and they replaced me! And off I charge, as fast as my little legs can take me. If that *#!*# thinks she's gonna have my part in this picture, she's got another thing coming. Mr. Carl chased after me, but I was a dog obsessed. I leapt onto that other dog and went right for her throat. Way I saw it, I was justified. She stole my part!

My stand-in <u>before</u> I finished with her. (Trust me, you don't want to see what she looked like after!)

Mr. Fleming to Judy: "Look sympathetic."

Mr. Fleming to Ray: "Look hopeful."

Mr. Fleming to me: "Look, don't eat the *#@*!* costume!"

Anyway, that usurper didn't put up a fight. Went instantly limp under me when I jumped her. I stopped a moment and looked down. Yep, I'd ripped open the throat, but there was just this white, fluffy stuff pouring out. And everybody was laughing.

And I got it. It's not a real dog. It's a stuffed item. And I laughed along with everybody else and gave them all a "I knew it wasn't a real dog" look. I don't think they were convinced though.

Mr. Fleming walked over and said, "Okay, that's our laugh for the day. Back to work." And back to work we went. I vowed never to miss a day of work ever. Ever. There might be a real dog lurking in the wings next time.

Excuse me, but while Maggie was taking the time to put me at ease concerning the Winkies, why did she fail to mention the Winged Monkeys!? Jiminy Crickets!!! It took every bit of willpower I had in my entire fifteen-pound body to hold it together when I got a gander at them.

I remember, about this time, I was starting to have some very serious concerns about this picture. It's supposed to be for kids but if they're anything like me, well, they'll take one look at Maggie and the Winkies and those monkeys and there won't be a dry seat in the house!

For me, the production ran smoothly for the next few weeks. We were finished with those

Sometimes it happens to us movie actors. You do some of your best work, and it ends up on the cutting room floor. Just look at that intensity, that concentration, that range of emotions happening all at once. (Judy, Ray and Jack are doing a good job, too!)

EDITOR'S NOTE: This scene, cut from The Wizard of Oz, found the Tin Man despondent over killing a bee.

MGM took a photo of every set in the picture so everybody would know where everything was supposed to be. Did you notice the poppy-design wallpaper? Nice touch.

Winged Monkeys and the Winkies, thank goodness. I refused to even look at the offending clod who stomped on my paw when we passed in the hall. Maybe that was small of me, but I had my pride.

Everyday, though, there seemed to be some new calamity on the set. Early on, Maggie had an accident involving fire. Buddy hadn't taken to his silver makeup and had been replaced by Jack. And, just as we were about to finish, we heard that Mr. Fleming had to go off to direct some Civil War epic (and we all know how they fare at the box office!). So we were to have yet another director.

I was a bit worried how all of this cine-matic chaos was going to cut together. But, I reminded myself, we can only give ourselves over to the process. And they probably have a very good editor. Let's pray.

So, we arrived at the final days of shoot-ing under the direction of Mr. Vidor. These would be the black-and-white segments. After all that Technicolor stuff, well, the Kansas set looked positively drab. Everywhere you looked gray and brown. Although everybody kept saying "sepia, sepia." You can dress it up with a fancy word, but brown is brown.

The first thing we shot on the Kansas set was the twister. Now, guess what they use to give the impression that a cyclone is coming? That's right. Wind machines.

And not one wind machine. Or two. Or even three. Eight blasted wind machines.

Well, you want to talk about not having to act a scene! They turned all those suckers on at once, and I could barely keep my feet on the stage floor. I was blown halfway to Sunday. And back. Again and again and again.

About this time, I was thinking, what does a little dog have to do to get out of this business!?

The next day, I was a total wreck. We're talking borderline nervous breakdown. But Mr. Carl assured me the storm sequence was over. That day, I was going to hear Judy sing. All I had to do was look at Judy.

You should all be so lucky! It was a lovely song. All about a rainbow. Judy was one scant bar into the song, and I'd forgotten about witches and Winkies and Winged Monkeys and, yep, wind machines, too. I just went along with little Judy's song and I forgot everything bad.

Oh, at one point I had to raise my paw — the

Despite the freezing-cold metal farm equipment where I was sitting, Judy's voice transported me over the rainbow. I know I'm not alone in this feeling, although I hope from where you're sitting, it's more comfy.

Here I am in a crossword puzzle I clipped from <u>Screen Romances Magazine</u> in August, 1939. I filled in as much as I could.

MOVIE X WORD PUZZLE

ACROSS

1. Where Dorothy lived before the cyclone
50. A garment for men worn close to the heart
51. Greek letter

DOWN

2. Miss Francis
3. Adrienne ----
3. Approaches
4. Randolph ---ott
5. Exclamation of surprise

47. Italian historian
48. Capital of West Honshu, Japan
49. Rouse
52. Snakelike fish
54. --- lie Burke
58. Sailor

—Sigue el camino de baldosas amarillas.
1060-72.2

When the movie was released in Spain, I suggested the caption: "Toto esta muy bonita." They didn't listen to me. Instead, they went with "Follow the yellow brick road." Original, huh?

Bravely they started up the Yellow Brick Road towards the Emerald City.... and magical adventure!

with
JUDY **GARLAND**
FRANK **MORGAN**
RAY **BOLGER**
BERT **LAHR**
JACK **HALEY**

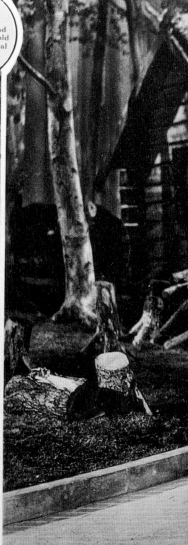

THE WIZ

Its METRO-

Yep, Judy, Ray and Jack look just dandy. I can't say it's my best angle.

ARD OF OZ
DWYN-MAYER'S TECHNICOLOR TRIUMPH!

COUNTRY OF ORIGIN U. S. A.

A bird's-eye, behind-the-scenes view of the Munchkinland sequence. I am dead center.

Opening night of <u>The Wizard of Oz</u> at Grauman's Chinese Theater in Hollywood. Mr. Carl and I are just pulling up, we were in the second car from the right.

previously Winkie-trampled paw — on cue.

Months later, when we went to the premiere, Mr. Carl and I were mortified to see that they used the take where I looked over toward him and anticipated the move! Now, probably, no one else noticed, but <u>we</u> did.

You give these movies your all and they select the worst takes!

I still hear "Over the Rainbow" on the radio. Sometimes it's Judy singing it, sometimes it's somebody else. I like some of the other versions but the original, well, you can't improve on perfection. Mr. Carl said that about me once and I was moved.

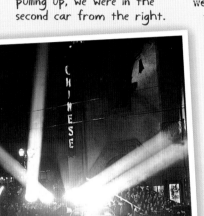

The wrap party for <u>The Wizard of Oz</u> was the best one yet. Mr. Carl had everybody in the cast sign my book. They said such sweet things to me, especially Judy. She picked me up and squeezed me tight. Not too tight. Some people are just born experts at the appropriate degree of holding tight.

Judy cried when Mr. Carl carried me away.

Nobody had ever cried before when I was taken away from them. Oh, I imagine my mother cried when I was taken away from her, but I don't like to think about that.

Mr. Carl and I drove home from MGM in silence. I should have been happy. The wrap party was such fun. But I was sort of sad. I fought back

Actually, I didn't, but it made for a nice story. Not that I wouldn't have liked to, mind you, but nobody thought of it until after the picture was over.

Our program from opening night.

"Hunden Toto" — that's me! (in Sweden)

DOUBLE FOR TOTO

Nothing will arouse interest among the youngsters more quickly than a pet stunt—and don't forget that the youngsters are going to supply an important part of your gross on "The Wizard." Toto, the two-year-old Cairn terrier who accompanies Dorothy on her journey to Oz, proves himself the greatest scene-stealer since Asta stopped the show in "The Thin Man." Any dog gag from a mutt show to a search for Toto's double will start talk and land newspaper space. Get the Tail-Waggers, S. P. C. A. and other organizations interested.

Billie Burke had to ...
...kle in a cast, her long di...
...uring "Bridal Suite," after finis...
wide search.

The 120 midgets playing Mund...

Toto, the dog, lived with Judy for two weeks before the picture started, to accustom him to his mistress throughout the picture.

Most colorful setting is Munch-kinland, containing 122 structures one-fourth normal size. It took a month to build and 150 painters worked to blend the 62 shades of all colors.

The 65 sets, if assembled one beside another, would cover 25 acres.

rsonerne:

Dorte	Judy Garland
...fessor Vupti	Frank Morgan
...er Fugleskræmsel ("Hunk")	Ray Bolger
...err Blikrud ("Zeke")	Bert Lahr
...ove Bangebuks ("Hickory")	Jack Haley
...teen Glinda	Billie Burke
...frøken Galde	Margaret Hamilton
...Onkel Henry	Charley Grapewin
...Nikko	Pat Walshe
...Tante Emm...	Clara Blandish

Hunden Toto og de glade Tumlinger

Udgiver af Metro-Goldwyn-Mayer A/S, Hammerichsgade 14, København V.
Redigeret af: Ray P. Nielsen.

TROLDMANDEN fra OZ
en METRO film

EDITOR'S NOTE: Miss Gulch prepares to take a very concerned Toto away. Interestingly, of the hundreds of official studio production stills, there are only three known for the Kansas sequence — this and two slight variant angles of the final scene. There were no official studio-issued stills for the "Over the Rainbow" song. At left is the brochure for the original Swedish release of the MGM movie, 1940.

EDITOR'S NOTE: Review from Harper's Bazaar, *August, 1939.*

— c'est moi!

tears and thought, what a wacky roller coaster of emotions this movie business can be. Well, came time for the premiere and believe-you-me I left my sad thoughts at home!

Mr. Carl took me to this big movie palace on Hollywood Boulevard called Grauman's Chinese Theater. That's where they have all those footprints of the stars in the cement in the courtyard.

Someone at the studio had made mention a few weeks before of me putting my paw prints in cement there, but it was never brought up again.

That happens a lot in the movie business. People get all excited and say stuff, and then they forget they ever said it. If you remind them, they usually get nasty and deny they ever said any such thing.

So I just hold my tongue. It's served me well.

Well, despite my reservations about some of the questionable takes they used in the finished film, I have to say I thought The Wizard of Oz

An Italian fan sent me this comic strip. I guess "Buh! Buh!" is Italian for "Bow! Wow!" I thought the artist captured my "Hooop...la!" very nicely although whatever "Hooop...la!" means I couldn't tell ya.

2

My cameo! Loved my sophisticated costume. I look good in white. Don't you agree?

The Kennel scene from <u>The Women</u>. What's wrong with this picture? Hint: I'M NOT IN IT!

EDITOR'S NOTES: ABOVE: Production still from The Women. *As these types of studio stills are usually taken during a rehearsal, Toto (who is very present in the finished sequence) was undoubtedly resting in her trailer when this was shot.* OPPOSITE: El Mago di Oz. *Italian comic book adaptation of* The Wizard of Oz, *1948.*

was really something! All that color and music and singing and happiness. And the scary parts were good, too. To me, the film-makers — every last one of 'em — found the perfect balance of innocence and danger. It truly lived up to the hype, and I was proud to be a tiny, furry lit-tle part of the bigger magic.

I was looking forward to a little vacation time after Oz but the suits at MGM had dif-ferent ideas. They'd already booked two more films for me.

I had waited a long time to be on the top of the canine heap and wasn't about to let

Another one of those publicist exaggerations. Featherbrain was no lady. His real name was Butch. And, trust me, he was no gentleman either!

being on a roll just, well, roll away. One can always sleep in the grave is what I thought at the time. So, Mr. Carl told the suits, "She's ready for her next close-up!"

The first role after Oz was a movie called <u>The Women</u> and everybody in the picture was going to be female. Even the dogs. Everywhere you looked — one gal after another!

I was so excited. I was in the first shot of the picture. Now, there used to be this movie convention that the star never appeared in the first shot of a movie. But I guess <u>this</u> star was about to defy that convention.

My excitement was a bit short-lived, however, after Mr. Carl flipped through the script and found out that I am, indeed, in the first shot of the picture but, apparently, I'm ONLY in the first scene of the picture.

But we have to take these disappointments in stride. I

When you're a star and courting the attention of the press, there's no limit to how silly you'll let them make you look. Witness, this photo.

IT'S GOT THE
HEART-THROB
of "BOYS TOWN"

Bad
LITTLE ANGEL

Virginia WEIDLER
GENE REYNOLDS
GUY KIBBEE
IAN HUNTER
ELIZABETH PATTERSON
REGINALD OWEN
HENRY HULL
LOIS WILSON

A Metro-Goldwyn-Mayer PICTURE

This is a lobby card and poster from a film I made with child star Virginia Weidler. Look how fat I look in the illustration below! A butterball with hair! I begged MGM to retouch the image but they insisted that I looked "healthy and well-fed" which, as I kept telling them, is NOT EXACTLY the kind of image an actress wants to project!

ANGEL

A Metro

My favorite photo of Virginia and me.

In <u>Bad Little Angel</u>, Virginia, Gene, and I ran the gamut of emotions from A...   ...to B.

always refer to <u>The Women</u> as the film in which I had my first cameo role. Only <u>stars</u> do cameos. If you aren't well-known and you only have one scene in a movie, you're a day-player. I had graduated out of that league, thank you very much!

My next movie was better suited to my talents. <u>Patsy</u> was the title although they later changed it to <u>Bad Little Angel</u>. It's all about a dog and a little girl. I know what you're thinking. We've seen this one before. But it was an entertaining variation on a well-trod theme.

EDITOR'S NOTE: Toto's character was also called 'Rags' in Bright Eyes.

Virginia was the little girl, and I played "Rags." And it was a good part. I got to go through a myriad of emotions.

I tried very hard to vary my head tilt responses in that picture, and I'm very proud of my work. If anything I hoped that the audience would look at this and Oz and say "I can't believe it's the same dog. Such artistic progress!"

Well, <u>The Wizard of Oz</u>, <u>The Women</u> and <u>Bad Little Angel</u> were all made within a year, and I don't mind telling you that I was bushed.

But, when you're a

* * *

Toto, the dog of "The Wizard of Oz" and now of "Bad Little Angel," not only is receiving fan mail but is being besieged by autograph hunters. Jack Weatherwax, its trainer, carries an inked stamp pad, and Toto affixes paw-prints to proffered autograph albums.

EDITOR'S NOTES: OPPOSITE: Bad Little Angel *re-used many of the 'wild tracks' of Toto's barking recorded for* The Wizard of Oz. *TOP: Child actor Gene Reynolds would go on to write and produce the smash TV series, M*A*S*H. ABOVE: Clipping from* Bad Little Angel *pressbook. When Carl Spitz was otherwise engaged on another movie, assistant trainer Jack Weatherwax filled in.*

© Vitagraph, Inc

TROUBLE'S AFLOAT when the debonair super-sleuth, James Stephenson, and
Edward Brophy smell a clue in "Calling Philo Vance," at the Strand Friday.

J

P

l

DOG BALLY STUNTS

COME ON IN AND SEE ME HELP PHILO VANCE SOLVE HIS MOST BAFFLING CASE !

Captain MacTavish, Philo Vance's Scottie mascot, tie in nicely
on many exploitation stunts. Place a small wool Scottie on
a table in the lobby. Underneath the table, concealed by a
curtain is a victrola. Have a wax recording made at some
music shop with copy along the lines as illustrated.

Make an effective street bal-
ly by having somebody,
dressed like Vance, walk a
Scottie pup through the
streets. Lettering on dog's
sweater reads: "I am Cap-
tain MacTavish, Philo
Vance's first assistant. See
us in action at the Strand."

Run a dog-checking booth
in your lobby. Hire some re-
sponsible kid, who won't get
lost, to take care of your pa-
trons' pooches while they're
attending the show. Decor-
ate the booth with doggy
stills available at your local
Vitagraph exchange.

(Lead)

'Calling Philo Van
At The Strand

Surprise mystery thrillers
have long been movie favorites.
And when it's an S. S. Van
Dine yarn, that means tops in
this type of story. The artistry
of Van Dine has been recognized
since ...

tional, is o...
been taken ...
paper head ...
intrigue an ...
national ...
around an ...
turer wh ...
cover ...

*Clippings from my days
on Calling Philo Vance.*

Beauty Care For Dogs

Jack Weatherwax, dog trainer for the animals which help
bring the murderer to justice in
"Calling Philo Vance," had to
manicure one of his dogs' nails
and brush the teeth of another
on the set. The little dog, Toto,
which though a female Cairn
terrier takes on the screen identity of Capt. MacTavish, a male
Scottie, in the film, had to have
her nails pared so they wouldn't
rattle and cause her to skid
when she padded swiftly and
noiselessly about the stylish
mansion in which an unidenti-
fied slayer had already disposed
of two victims. The bigger dog,
Kazan, a police dog which finally
knocked the slayer to the ground
and tore at his neck, had to
have his teeth brushed after
each "take" because the actor
who played the slayer wore
heavily padded arms and shoul-
ders on his coat, and the latter
yielded short lengths of horse
hair that got between Kazan's
teeth. Between scenes the dog's
antics amused the whole crew.

Warner Bros.-First National.

Busy Terrier Pup
In New Strand Film

The 17-ounce Cairn terrier,
Toto, whose curious nose turns
up one clew after another in the
Warner Bros. mystery thriller
"Calling Philo Vance," the film
now at the Strand, has a curious
but very busy record in films.

Toto has played everything
from a Sealyham (disguised by
a bath in whitening fluid) to a
black Scottie, which she imper-
sonates in her current role. In
fact, Toto despite her sex, plays
a very masculine little Scottie,
named Capt. MacTavish, with
James Stephenson as her master,
the great detective, in the Philo
Vance film.

Toto began her film career as
a wee puppy, more full of pep
than knowledge, but willing to
learn, in Shirley Temple's
"Bright Eyes," three years ago.
She recently completed another
triumph as Judy Garland's dog,
Terry, in "Wizard of Oz."

The canine is a kennel mate
of Buck, the $500 a week St.
Bernard, and of Prince, the
fighting fool of a great Dane
which has chewed up packs of
timber wolves in a succession of
far north films. Among this
rugged company, little button
eyed Toto reigns as queen of
the kennels owned by Carl Spitz,
whose specialty is renting canines to the screen. All Toto
need do is look roguishly at
Buck, and snarl commandingly
at Prince, and she gets peace
and quiet among the forty vari-
egated pooches in the Carl Spitz
dog quarters.

THERE'S ONLY ONE MAN WHO CAN SOLVE THIS MURDER!

...and one DOG, thank
you very much!

star there's the press avalanche to contend with. I remember Judy saying once: "They don't pay you to make the movie. They pay you for the press junket afterwards." And right she was. Such work! Such tedium!

The publicist and two photographers came out to the kennel for a special shoot. Buck only had one photographer when Mr. Gable was here. Of course, I'm too much of a lady to remind him, but I could tell he was impressed.

Oh, and something else even more significant happened around that time. I had done three back-to-back pictures at MGM, and I'd worked with many of the same department heads and crew and everyone had taken to calling me "Toto." Hardly anyone ever called me Terry anymore.

One day, Mr. Carl said, "Come here, Terry. Come here, girl!"

I didn't respond. So Mr. Carl sat me down and said that, to avoid identity confusion, from then on I'd be known as "Toto."

Toto. I liked the sound of that. Still do.

In a way, though, I was a little sad to leave old Terry behind. But, ultimately, Cary Grant was happy he left behind "Archibald Leach." And I know Judy was happy to jettison "Frances Gumm." Wouldn't you be!?

I made two pictures the following year. A stinker called Son of the Navy, which was another Monogram picture. A step down from MGM glory if you ask me, but Mr. Carl says you have to take employment as it comes. Careers are fickle.

They were nicer to us this time at Monogram but, oh, those shooting schedules! How could they expect a dog to do good work when they treat you like, well, a dog?

My next picture was a vast improvement and my first for Warner Brothers. At this rate, I thought, I'll be the dog who's been had by all the studios.

The picture was called Calling Philo Vance. It was my first remake. The first version was called The Kennel Murder Case. A kennel? Hmm. Wonder how I got the part? It was a very satisfying experience. I played "MacTavish." At first, I thought they must've confused me with a Scottie.

Actually, one of my newest best friends at Mr. Carl's kennel was a Scottie named Mr. Binkie. I remember thinking Warners might have made a mistake and hired me instead of him for Calling Philo Vance, what with the character name and all.

But I certainly wasn't going to set them straight. It's dog-eat-dog in the movie business. And besides, Mr. Binkie was doing okay. He had been in an "A" picture or two himself. Even if they weren't in color!

In Calling Philo Vance, yours truly is instrumental in solving a crime. James — who plays the detective — told me at the wrap party that he couldn't have done it without me. Who am I to argue!?

Twin Beds found me back at United Artists. Some things had changed, though. There were three suits at the first meeting, but one of them

Here I am taking Musty's photo. A confession: the studio set this up to look like I was taking his picture with a Brownie. Everybody knows I use a Rollie.

used to work at Paramount, one at Fox and the other — shudder, shudder — at Monogram.

Seems that these suits sort of rotate. They stay at one studio for awhile, make a lot of mistakes but very few decisions, and then move to another studio. Curious.

You can play mean, but you're not mean. I can play scared, but I'm not scared. (It's called acting.)

Remember when I said that at wrap parties, everybody says they'll see each other again but it hardly ever happens? Well, in Twin Beds, I again worked with my old friend Maggie — the Wicked Witch from Oz! She played a maid in this one — no green makeup but she did wear a lot of black. And, inbetween takes, she did her Witch cackle for me. It didn't scare me anymore, though. Made me laugh.

I have to admit, I was one pretty well-known pooch by this time. People would come by the kennel to see Toto, and Mr. Carl would trot me out. Very willingly on my part. I hate to disappoint my audience.

I'd do a little routine for the vis-

EDITOR'S NOTE: Margaret Hamilton and Toto in Twin Beds, 1942.

I worked it out. That breaks down to twenty grand a pooch. Not bad!

Six movie dogs valued at $120,000 in Chicago for stage appearance. Left to right, with pictures in which they starred: Promise, pointer, "The Biscuit Eater"; Buck, St. Bernard, "Call of the Wild"; Toto, Cairn terrier (front), "Wizard of Oz"; Musty, English mastiff, "Swiss Family Robinson"; Prince Carl, Great Dane, "Wuthering Heights" and Mr. Binkie, scotty, "The Light That Failed."
[TRIBUNE Photo.]

Lounging with Musty in the summer of 1940.

Top billing!

In our driveway just before we hit the road for our 1942 tour. I have no idea what everyone was looking at but I was a seasoned professional by then and knew how to find the lens.

itors. It didn't seem to matter
what I did. I was a star by
then and could get a tremendous reaction from not doing
very much at all!

Also, about this time, Mr.
Carl took us on the road for
a personal appearance tour.

Me and Mr. Binkie. He was
one handsome Scottie!

I was famous, of course,
and so were Buck and Mr.
Binkie. Prince had done
some very good work over
at Goldwyn. We would do
stage shows to great
acclaim before the movies
and, one time, the manag-
er came running to tell
us that the featured picture was one
of my movies and so was the sup-
porting one!

I was so excited that I couldn't
wait to get through our show. I even
skipped a couple of encores just to
move everything along.

Afterwards, Mr. Carl, Mr. Binkie,
Buck, Prince, and I each took a seat
in the theater to watch me on the
big screen.

I should have known, though. We
were playing some dive in downtown Yuma, and
it was a Monogram double-bill of Barefoot Boy
and Son of the Navy. I hid under my seat when
the credits came on.

The other dogs never let me forget that
afternoon. Sometimes, I guess fate just has
to throw you a curve. It's humbling.

Easy to Look At ended up being my last
movie. Don't really know why. One day the
phone just stopped ringing. It happens I'm
told. And, to be perfectly honest, I wasn't
the same dog anymore. Oh, I was okay in the
head. I wasn't going dotty or anything. But I

EDITOR'S NOTE: Mr. Binkie
played an important role in
the Ronald Coleman film,
The Light that Failed.
Probably because Toto was
photographed side-by-side
with Mr. Binkie in many
publicity photos and they
were similar breeds, it is often
erroneously reported that Toto
starred in the Coleman film.

couldn't seem to run as fast or as far. Or jump as high. Sometimes, in the morning, it took a bit more effort to pick myself up out of bed. But, you know what? I wasn't sad about any of this. I really and truly didn't mind.

Sure, I loved the excitement and the glamour of making movies, but I was luckier than many. I have what most movie stars don't. A happy home life. I love my home and the people who care for me. And they do care for me. And I for them. And, no, it's not just because they feed me. Although that's a nice bonus!

There are always smiles and food and laughter and food and petting and food and petting. As far as I am concerned, our routine has been perfected and can go on forever.

I'm not very old in people years but, in dog years, I'm pushing 70. I'm slowing down. I think Mr. Carl notices this. I get picked up a lot more often and held longer. And, I figure, why walk when you can ride?

Some of my friends went away. We lost Buck and Prince. They are buried at the back of the property. Mrs. Carl cried each time. Me, too.

But Mr. Binkie is still around. He now shares my bed under the sink. But, don't worry, he's a gentleman. The day he took up residence in the basket, he told me that the vet did something to him early on that made him not be a serious threat to the ladies. Something about removing some equipment. But I can see into Mr. Binkie's true soul — even with equipment he would be a gentleman.

Mr. Carl still works very hard. There are new dogs that come — new stars. And before you go thinking it — no, there's no jealousy on my part. Because we're all treated the same here. To Mr. Carl, we're all stars.

The Spitz family has that rare gift. They know how to parcel out equal amounts of love. It's not like they use a measuring cup, it's just something they know in their hearts.

DOROTHY lived in the midst of the great Kansas prairies, with her Uncle Henry and Aunt Em and her little dog Toto. One day the north and south winds met where their house stood, and made it the center of a cyclone.

I had a good morning today. I finished off two bowls of cereal, did my business, took the first dozen or so of my daily naps.

When I woke, Mr. Carl was listening to the radio. It seems that all is not well with the world outside our kennel. Mr. Carl talks of loud noises back in his homeland. Loud noises he wishes would stop. I guess those loud noises are sort of his own private wind machines.

It looked to me like he was going to cry, but then the man on the radio stopped and they played a song. And wouldn't you know it? It was "Over the Rainbow," and it was my Judy singing. Mr. Carl cheered up and smiled.

I cried, though. Don't know why.

I'm almost finished with my book. The one you're reading. If anyone ever does read this! If anyone cares about the ramblings of a little dog called Toto.

A final note to the reader: I explained earlier how I learned to read. I imagine you're wondering how a dog knows how to write. Well, let me tell you...I'm keeping that one to myself! A girl has to retain some mystery.

Truly, I'd like to think someone might care to read this someday, but I'm a realist. Movie stars come and movie stars go. I may be forgotten some day and, you know, that'll be just fine. I remember me!

I said at the start I was doing this mostly for myself anyway and that's the truth. I'm going to finish before the end of the day, check the spelling and the punctuation (with an eye on preserving my own special voice) and put it in a box. Right before dusk, I'll bury it in the back somewhere near Buck and Prince. I know they'll keep watch over it.

Right before lunch, it rained. Poured. I waited out the deluge under the Buick next to the garage. It let up after awhile. The dark clouds and the gray skies went away almost immediately, and the sun shined bright. Suddenly, there were all sorts of colors. Sorta like that part in <u>The Wizard of Oz</u> where it went from black-and-white — pardon me, <u>sepia</u> — to color. The golden sun glistened on the orange trees, and the air smelled like rose water.

I stood there in the middle of the yard and looked around at everything and smiled. My tail wagged uncontrollably. This, I thought, <u>this</u> is the life!

Then, I headed into the kitchen. It was way past my lunchtime.

Oh, I almost forgot. Before I went inside, I chased a rainbow!

THE END

AFTERWORD

FROM KODACHROME BY JUIMET

Toto, a.k.a. Terry, died sometime towards the end of World War II.

She was buried in the backyard of Carl Spitz's Hollywood Dog Training School. Buried but certainly not forgotten.

For Toto—both the character and the performer—is one of the many reasons why we went to Oz in the first place and why we're so eager to return.

Outside of movies, in our "real lives," the bond between guardian and pet is a bond that transcends the commonplace. No matter what the complexities of the day, we allow ourselves to reduce a moment or two to a refreshingly simplistic essence.

I love you. You love me.

No conditions. No expectations.

But such joy.

I had always wanted to think that a dog like Toto might share my feelings. Now, I'm certain she did.

Because, well, we have her word for it.

—Willard Carroll

THE MOVIES OF TOTO A.K.A. TERRY

BRIGHT EYES
(Fox Film Corporation—1934)
Director: David Butler
Cast: Shirley Temple,
Jane Withers, James Dunn,
Terry as 'Rags'

READY FOR LOVE
(Paramount—1934)
Director: Marion Gering
Richard Arlen, Ida Lupino,
Terry as a dog

DARK ANGEL
(United Artists—1935)
Director: Sidney Franklin
Cast: Fredric March,
Merle Oberon,
Terry as a dog

FURY
(MGM—1936)
Director: Fritz Lang
Cast: Spencer Tracey,
Sylvia Sidney,
Terry as 'Rainbow'

THE BUCCANEER
(Paramount—1938)
Director: Cecil B. DeMille
Cast: Fredric March,
Walter Brennan,
Terry as a dog

BAREFOOT BOY
(Monogram—1938)
Director: Karl Brown
Cast: Jackie Moran,
Terry as 'Terry'

THE WIZARD OF OZ
(MGM—1939)
Director: Victor Fleming
Cast: Judy Garland,
Terry as 'Toto'

THE WOMEN
(MGM—1939)
Director: George Cukor
Cast: Norma Shearer,
Joan Crawford,
Toto as a dog

BAD LITTLE ANGEL
(MGM—1939)
Director: William Thiele
Cast: Virginia Weidler,
Gene Reynolds,
Toto as 'Rags'

SON OF THE NAVY
(Monogram—1940)
Director: William Nigh
Cast: James Dunn,
Jean Parker,
Toto as a dog

**CALLING
PHILO VANCE**
(Warner Bros.—1940)
Director: William Clemens
Cast: James Stephenson,
Margo Stevenson,
Toto as 'MacTavish'

**THE CHOCOLATE
SOLDIER**
(MGM—1941)
Director: Roy Del Ruth
Cast: Nelson Eddy,
Risë Stevens,
Toto as a dog

TWIN BEDS
(United Artists—1942)
Director: Tim Whelan
Cast: George Brent,
Joan Bennett,
Toto as 'Poochie'

EASY TO LOOK AT
(Universal—1945)
Director: Ford Beebe
Cast: Gloria Jean,
Kirby Grant,
Toto as a dog

Toto a.k.a. Terry undoubtedly appeared in other films during her career but, as Toto never mentions any others by name in her memoir, they must not have been of much consequence.

EDITOR'S NOTE: Illustration by Dale Ulrey from The Wizard of Oz, *1956.*

Terry,
mein Schatze!
Fritz

Dearest Terry:
You are 'Toto'!
Frank would be so proud.
Maud

Terry:
There's not much
meat on your bones
but what there is
is cherce!
Spence

Dear Toto—
I think I'll
miss you most
of all (don't
tell Ray!)
Judy